TELL ME WHY, TELL ME HOW

WHY DO VOLCANOES ERUPT?

WIL MARA

 **Marshall Cavendish**
Benchmark
New York

Marshall Cavendish Corporation
99 White Plains Road
Tarrytown, NY 10591-5502
www.marshallcavendish.us

All websites were available and accurate when this book was sent to press.

Library of Congress Cataloging-in-Publication Data
Mara, Wil.
Why do volcanoes erupt? / by Wil Mara.
p. cm. — (Tell me why, tell me how)
Includes index.
ISBN 978-0-7614-3989-9
1. Volcanic eruptions—Juvenile literature. 2. Volcanoes—Juvenile literature. I. Title.

QE521.3.M29 2010
551.21—dc22

2008029431

Photo research by Candlepants Incorporated

Cover Photo: George Steinmetz / Corbis

The photographs in this book are used by permission and through the courtesy of:
Corbis: Theo Allofs, 1; Ashely Jouhar/zefa, 8; Visuals Unlimited, 10; Reuters, 22. Getty Images: Fredrik Clement, 4; Bobby Haas, 17. Alamy Images: Michael Griffin, 5; foodfolio, 13; David Ball, 16; Travel Pix, 20. Photo Researchers Inc.: Mehau Kulyk, 6; Gary Hincks, 9, 18; Mikkel Juul Jensen, 12; David Hardy, 14; Bernhard Edmaier, 16. U.S. Geological Survey: 23. National Oceanic and Atmospheric Administration: 24. The Bridgeman Art Library: Private Collection, 25.

Editor: Joy Bean
Publisher: Michelle Bisson
Art Director: Anahid Hamparian
Series Designer: Alex Ferrari

Printed in Malaysia

1 3 5 6 4 2

CONTENTS

There is more going on beneath your feet than you might imagine.

Far Beneath Your Feet

When you stand outside, do you ever think about what is beneath your feet? If you are on a sidewalk, you probably think it is only concrete. If you are standing on the beach, you might think it is just sand. But what is farther down? Is there more concrete, or more sand? And what is underneath a lake or an ocean? There must be something down there, right?

Our planet is made up of three main layers: the **crust**, the **mantle**, and the **core**. The crust is the outermost layer— the one we see every day. We walk on it, play on it, and build roads and houses on it. If you dig a hole in the dirt, you are digging into the Earth's crust. In order to dig down far enough to reach the

This groundhog's hole may look deep, but you would have to dig a lot deeper to get to the bottom of the Earth's crust.

bottom of the crust, you would have to go anywhere from 3 to almost 50 miles (4.8 to 80 kilometers). That might sound like a long way, but the crust is, in fact, the thinnest of the three layers.

After the crust comes the mantle. The mantle is the thickest layer, with an average depth of about 1,700 miles (2,750 km). To give you an idea of how much that is, here is a comparison: if you were in a car going 65 miles (104.6 km) an hour (a brisk highway speed) and made no stops, it would take you almost 26 hours—slightly more than a full day—to go from the top of the mantle to the bottom. The mantle is also a fairly hot place, with temperatures reaching as high as 6,750 degrees Fahrenheit (3,732 degrees Celsius). Compare that to the mere 375 °F (190.5 °C) you need to

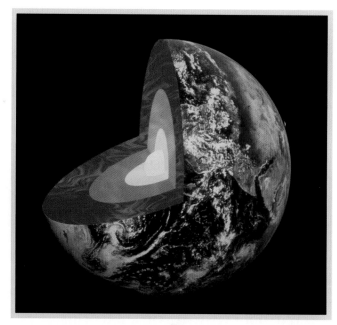

A cut-away of the Earth shows the crust (red), the mantle (orange), the outer core (yellow) and the inner core (white).

cook a steak on a barbecue! The mantle is composed mostly of solid rock, but there are parts where the heat and pressure are so high that the rock turns into a thick liquid.

Now I Know!

What are the three main layers of the Earth, starting with the one we see every day?

Crust, mantle, and core.

Finally, there is the core. Just as its name implies, it makes up the very center of our planet. It has a thickness of about 2,150 miles (3,460 km) and consists of two parts: the inner core and the outer core. Scientists believe that the inner core is solid and made of heavy metals such as iron and nickel, whereas in the outer core is more hot, thick fluid. The core has the highest temperatures of the three layers, ranging anywhere from 7,000 to 9,000 °F (3,870 to 4,980 °C). The Earth's core is so hot that scientists have been unable to retrieve any material from it to study. There are no containers able to hold core samples that hot without burning up!

Rocks are very hard substances,
but they are turned to liquid
when the temperature and
pressure are high enough.

 Red-Hot

Imagine holding a rock in your hand and giving it a good squeeze. It is pretty hard, right? Maybe you have heard the phrase "solid as a rock"? Hard, solid, and tough are all good words for describing rocks. Now try to imagine this— deep inside the Earth, rock sometimes turns into liquid. And this liquid— which is very important in volcanic activity—is called **magma**.

Most magma is created in the area between the Earth's crust and the mantle. This is an area with a very high temperature. It is also an area of great pressure. When the temperature and pressure

Liquid magma, shown here in yellow, forms inside the Earth.

9

reach a certain point, the normally solid rock cannot take the pressure and heat any longer and it begins to melt. It is similar to the melting of a candle. Before it is lit, the candle is solid, but after the heat of the flame touches it, it slowly melts into liquid.

Magma can still contain pieces of solid rock. This is because some of the minerals in a rock melt at higher temperatures than others. This creates a mixture of glowing,

Granite is a common type of igneous rock, which is formed when liquid magma cools and hardens.

syrupy magma and darker chunks of harder material. Also, magma that cools and hardens before reaching the surface creates a new type of rock called igneous rock. A body of igneous rock is called a pluton, named after Pluto, the ancient Roman god of the underworld. Granite is a common type of pluton—you may even have some granite in your home.

This illustration shows how magma begins to rise as rock melts. Floating gas bubbles drive the magma upwards.

A High-Pressure Situation

As rock melts into magma, it becomes lighter and begins to rise through the Earth's crust. It is also pushed up by gases that have become mixed in during the melting process. These gases act like bubbles in soda, which rise because they are lighter than the soda itself.

Magma is a thick, slow-moving fluid, which means it has a high **viscosity**. In simple terms, the thicker a fluid is, the more viscosity it has. Honey, for example, has a high viscosity, so it flows slowly, whereas ordinary water does not have a high viscosity, so it flows quickly.

Magma flows and honey are similar in that they both have a high viscosity. That means they are slow-moving fluids.

The viscosity of magma varies, but it is never as low as ordinary water.

   As magma rises, it makes its way through the Earth's crust in every available crack and crevice. The extreme heat of the magma will widen these passageways and sometimes creates

Magma that continues to grow must find a place to gather, and that place is called a magma chamber. The magma chamber, as seen in these illustrations, grows beneath the Earth's surface.

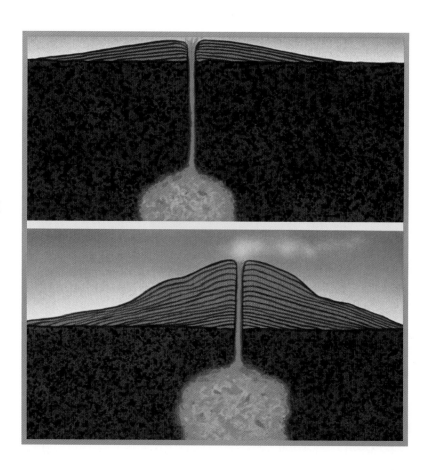

new ones. If the magma
does not find any more
passages, it will gather in
a space called a **magma
chamber**. The magma
will continue to gather

until the pressure in the chamber reaches an explosive point.
Many of the world's most active volcanoes lie directly over
magma chambers that are continually filled with magma from
activities in the crust and mantle below them.

When the pressure in a magma chamber becomes too high, the magma forces itself upwards
with a great amount of force.

A volcano looks very much like any other mountain. However, volcanoes have a hole in the top from past eruptions.

A Hole in the Ground

You may already have an idea of what a volcano looks like—similar to a mountain, except the top is flattened, and a hole is there instead of a point.

But this is only one type of volcano. A volcano might also look like a plateau, which is a raised area of land that's wide and flat on top. It can have the craterlike appearance of an empty lake. Or it can simply be a series of steam-spewing cracks and holes in the ground.

This is a bird's eye view of a volcano with a wide, craterlike top.

What all volcanoes have in common, however, is at least one opening that goes into the Earth's crust. This is called the **vent**, and it can be located anywhere on a volcano's outer body. Like the volcanoes themselves, the vents can have different appearances. They can look like rips or cracks

This illustration shows that all volcanoes have one thing in common—a passageway that runs into the Earth. Magma flows through this passageway.

(fissures) in the Earth's surface or roundish holes. They are located at the top of the **conduit**.

Not all volcanoes are "alive." Some have stopped erupting altogether and will likely never erupt again. Scientists use three main categories to classify volcanoes: active, dormant, and extinct. An active volcano is one that has erupted recently or may erupt very soon. A dormant volcano is considered to be "sleeping." It is not active, but is still dangerous and could erupt in the near

This is an active volcano with a lake in its crater. Sometimes volcanoes sit dormant for so long that their vents become plugged (with soil, rocks, etc.) and lakes form in the craters.

future. An extinct volcano has not erupted in hundreds of years and shows no signs of volcanic activity.

About fifty volcanoes erupt each year worldwide. Possibly the most well-known volcano in the United States is Mount St. Helens in Washington state. In 1980, the mountain erupted,

Diamond Head, a dormant volcano located in Honolulu, Hawaii, has not erupted for 150,000 years, so many people consider it extinct.

and it became the largest volcanic eruption in the continental United States. The blast was so strong that within fifteen minutes of erupting, a cloud of ash and gas had risen 15 miles (24 km) into the air.

Now I Know!
What do all volcanoes have in common?

A passageway for magma that runs deep into the Earth.

This is an extinct volcano located on Maupiti, an island near Tahiti.

This volcano has erupted and is spewing rock and ash into the air.

Why Do Volcanoes Erupt?

A volcanic eruption begins with the formation of magma in the lower sections of the Earth's crust and the upper region of the mantle. With pressure driving the magma, it travels upward with tremendous force. If it is halted in a magma chamber, the pressure will begin to increase. Eventually, the solid rock and other material surrounding the chamber will crack, creating a new passage to the Earth's surface. The magma will then flow through this conduit until it reaches the

This volcanic eruption is spewing lava into the air.

surface, where it will spew out in a volcanic eruption. Once magma reaches the air, it is called **lava**.

There are two main types of volcanic eruptions: **explosive** and **nonexplosive**. The one that you may know best is the first—explosive. It is certainly the most impressive to watch (from a safe distance, of course). Explosive eruptions occur when the pressure builds to a point where it throws both liquid and solid material into the air. The material is often thrown hundreds of yards or even miles from the vent. If a conduit has become plugged with hardened lava from previous eruptions, the explosion may be even worse once the plug gives way. There have even been explosions so powerful that they blew off large portions of the volcanic mountain.

Lava is thick and extremely hot.

Explosive eruptions are usually preceded by a rumbling or quaking, followed by an ear-piercing boom. These eruptions can last for hours or even days. They are also, of course, the most dangerous type of eruption. Explosive eruptions can send lava flowing into nearby towns, and they can create ash clouds that alter weather patterns. Ash clouds can make breathing difficult, and interfere with planes that fly too close.

Nonexplosive eruptions are gentler and safer. Magma simply rises to the Earth's surface with a minimum of pressure, and the lava flows out in a bubbling, glowing mass that eventually hardens into rock.

One of the most famous explosive eruptions in history was that of the Roman volcano Mount Vesuvius,

This painting shows Mount Vesuvius erupting back in 79 CE.

which blew in 79 CE and destroyed the two nearby cities of Pompeii and Herculaneum. Pompeii was so deeply buried under volcanic material that it essentially disappeared until it was accidentally rediscovered almost 1,700 years later. Mount Vesuvius is still considered active—and dangerous—today.

Activity

Make Your Own Volcano

This is a fun and easy science project that will enable you to create your own volcano from common household items. An adult should help you with every step, and you should make sure you have plenty of paper towels or newspapers in case there is too much of a mess from your eruption! (You may even want to consider doing the last step outside.)

What You Will Need

* Two-liter plastic bottle
* Spare plank of wood (plywood will do) about three feet square
* Papier-mâché
* Measuring cup and teaspoon
* Dishwashing liquid
* Baking soda (not baking powder)

* Red food coloring (optional)
* White vinegar

What to Do

1. Place the plastic bottle in the center of the wood plank, then build a mountain around it with the papier-mâché. The bottle cap should be off, because the opening will act as your volcano's vent. Make sure the papier-mâché is packed tightly around the bottle hole but is not covering it.

2. Dry your mountain fully overnight.

3. Combine one teaspoon of dishwashing liquid and one teaspoon of baking soda in a cup. You can also add a few drops of red food coloring to make the mixture look more lavalike.

4. Once it is all mixed, pour it into the open hole of the plastic bottle.

5. Now pour a quarter cup of white vinegar into the hole, and stand back! Your volcano should erupt almost instantly.

 Glossary

conduit—Underground passageway through which magma travels to reach the Earth's surface during a volcanic eruption.

core—The innermost and deepest layer of the Earth. There are two main parts: the outer core (molten) and the inner core (solid).

crust—The thinnest and outermost layer of the Earth. We live on the crust.

explosive—Forceful volcanic eruption that throws lava, rock, and ash into the air.

lava—The name for magma once it reaches the air during a volcanic eruption.

magma—Molten rock formed deep within the Earth. It is lighter than the still-solid rock around it, so it floats up to the Earth's surface and causes volcanic eruptions.

magma chamber—Underground space that becomes filled with molten magma. Magma chambers are commonly found beneath active volcanoes.

mantle—The middle and thickest layer of the Earth. It is mostly solid, but magma often forms in the area between the mantle and the crust.

nonexplosive—A gentle form of a volcanic eruption, where lava usually flows and bubbles out through a vent in a nonviolent fashion.

vent—Any opening in the Earth's surface through which volcanic activity occurs. The hole of a volcano.

viscosity—The amount of resistance to flow in a fluid or semifluid.

Find Out More

BOOKS

Bauer, Marion Dane. *Volcano!* (Natural Disasters). New York, NY: Aladdin Books, 2008.

Ganeri, Anita. *Volcano!* (Nature's Fury). London, England: Arcturus Publishing, 2007.

Lindeen, Mary. *Anatomy of a Volcano* (Shockwave: Science). New York, NY: Scholastic Library Publishing, 2007.

O'Meara, Donna. *Into the Volcano: A Volcano Researcher at Work.* Tonawanda, NY: Kids Can Press, 2007.

van Rose, Susanna. *Volcanoes & Earthquakes* (DK Eyewitness Books). New York, NY: DK Children's Books, 2008.

WEB SITES

U.S. government's FEMA Web site for kids about volcanoes
http://www.fema.gov/kids/volcano.htm

Discovery Kids' page about volcanoes and the Roman town of Pompeii
http://kids.discovery.com/games/pompeii/pompeii.html

National Geographic for Kids' page about volcanoes
http://www.nationalgeographic.com/ngkids/0312/

Index

Page numbers in **boldface** are illustrations.